Contents

Think like a scientist

Scientists look for information to understand our world. Information helps them to test ideas and solve problems. To think like a scientist, you need to look for information.

Pebble Plus

Working Scientifically

FINDING INFORMATION AND MAKING ARGUMENTS

by Riley Flynn

Raintree is an imprint of Capstone Global Library Limited, a company incorporated in England and Wales
having its registered office at 264 Banbury Road, Oxford, OX2 7DY – Registered company number: 6695582

www.raintree.co.uk
myorders@raintree.co.uk
Text © Capstone Global Library Limited 2018
The moral rights of the proprietor have been asserted.

Edited by Anna Butzer
Designed by Sarah Bennett
Picture research by Eric Gohl
Production by Laura Manthe

ISBN 978 1 4747 2257 5 (hardback)
20 19 18 17 16
10 9 8 7 6 5 4 3 2 1

ISBN 978 1 4747 2281 0 (paperback)
21 20 19 18 17
10 9 8 7 6 5 4 3 2 1

British Library Cataloguing in Publication Data
A full catalogue record for this book is available from the British Library.

Every effort has been made to contact copyright holders of material reproduced in this book. Any omissions
will be rectified in subsequent printings if notice is given to the publisher.

All the internet addresses (URLs) given in this book were valid at the time of going to press. However, due
to the dynamic nature of the internet, some addresses may have changed, or sites may have changed or
ceased to exist since publication. While the author and publisher regret any inconvenience this may cause
readers, no responsibility for any such changes can be accepted by either the author or the publisher.

Acknowledgements
Capstone: 9, 11; Shutterstock: Becky Sheridan, 17, Ivan Kuzmin, 19, Kdonmuang, 7, kozzi, 20,
Monkey Business Images, 13, overcrew, 15, PointImages, 5, wavebreakmedia, cover
Design Elements: Shutterstock

Printed and bound in the United Kingdom.

Where can you find information?

You can read a book or

an online article. You can also

watch a video about a topic.

Information is all around us.

Use text features

Text features can help you find

key information. Start by

reading the contents page.

Then look for headings,

bold print and text boxes.

World of giants

The **dinosaurs** were a group of animals that lived millions of years ago. Some dinosaurs were the biggest animals that ever walked on Earth. *Apatosaurus* was 23 metres long, about twice as long as a bus. The hunter *Saurophaganax* was 11 metres long, more than twice as long as a car.

Saurophaganax

Apatosaurus

Torosaurus had the largest head of any land animal. It was 2.4 metres long. That's longer than an average bed!

Torosaurus

Pictures also hold information.
You are reading about dinosaurs.
What do the different dinosaurs
look like? Do the pictures have
labels? These features help you
to understand the text.

The long neck

One of the longest **dinosaurs** was a **sauropod** called *Diplodocus*. It grew to be 27 metres long. That is longer than the length of a swimming pool. Sauropods lived in herds. The younger animals walked in the centre where they could be protected by the larger, older dinosaurs.

Did you know?
Some sauropods, such as *Saltasaurus*, had bone **armour** on their backs to protect them from attack.

Diplodocus

Saltasaurus

14

15

Facts and evidence

Gathering information helps you to build an argument. To argue about a topic you need to know facts. We can prove a fact to be true.

Arguments need facts. You may say that we should not throw rubbish into a river. Why not? Fish may think the rubbish is food. Our rubbish can harm fish. That is a fact.

Every argument also has two parts. The first part is a claim. The claim is the main point. You can claim that some animals see well in the dark.

The second part of an argument
is evidence. You have observed
bats flying and eating in the
dark. This evidence proves
your claim.

Finding information and making claims

Which food will attract the most insects at a picnic? Find out!

What you need:

- pencil
- paper
- honey
- bread
- hot dog, cut up into small pieces
- 3 jam jar lids
- ruler
- timer, clock or watch
- a dry or sunny day

What to do:

1. Draw three columns on the piece of paper.
   List the items of food – one in each column.

2. Place a small amount of each food on a jam
   jar lid. Put the lids outside. Place the lids about
   10 centimetres apart.

3. Observe the lids. Write down the time you start
   watching the lids.

4. Each time an insect inspects a food, draw a tick in
   its column. Also write down the type of insect.

5. How long did it take for each food to attract its
   first insect? Add this information to each column.

What do you think now?

Make a claim. A claim is something you believe to
be true. Which type of food will attract the most
insects at a picnic? Why? Now share what you have
learned with a friend.

Glossary

argument set of reasons to support an idea

claim say that something is true

evidence information that helps to prove something is true or false

fact information that is truthful and correct

gather collect things

label word or phrase that describes something

observe watch someone or something closely in order to learn about it

problem something that raises questions

Read more

365 Science Activities (Usborne Activities),
(Usborne Publishing, 2014)

Experiments with Light (Read and Experiment),
Isabel Thomas (Raintree, 2015)

Websites

www.bbc.co.uk/bitesize/ks1/science
Enjoy some fun activities and learn more about science.

www.dkfindout.com/uk/science
Find out more about science and famous scientists.

Comprehension questions

1. What is a fact?

2. Look at the pictures on pages 9 and 11. What text features can you see?

Index